EDGE
T0080553

U.S. MARINES by the Numbers

by Elizabeth Raum

Consultant: Raymond L. Puffer, PhD
Historian, Retired
Edwards Air Force Base History Office

CAPSTONE PRESS
a capstone imprint

Edge Books are published by Capstone Press,
1710 Roe Crest Drive, North Mankato, Minnesota 56003
www.capstonepub.com

Copyright © 2014 by Capstone Press, a Capstone imprint. All rights reserved.
No part of this publication may be reproduced in whole or in part, or stored in a retrieval system, or transmitted in any form or by any means, electronic, mechanical, photocopying, recording, or otherwise, without written permission of the publisher.

Library of Congress Cataloging-in-Publication Data
Raum, Elizabeth.
U.S. Marines by the numbers / by Elizabeth Raum.
pages cm. — (Edge. Military by the numbers)
Includes bibliographical references and index.
Summary: "Describes aspects of the U.S. Marines using numbers, stats, and infographics"— Provided by publisher.
Audience: Grades 4 to 6.
ISBN 978-1-4765-3919-5 (library binding)
ISBN 978-1-4765-5122-7 (paperback)
ISBN 978-1-4765-5967-4 (eBook PDF)
1. United States. Marine Corps—Juvenile literature. I. Title.
VE23.R42 2014
359.9′60973—dc23 2013032522

* Numbers based on 2013 information unless otherwise noted

Editorial Credits
Mandy Robbins and Brenda Haugen, editors; Heidi Thompson, designer; Danielle Ceminsky, production specialist

Photo Credits
AP Images: Joe Rosenthal, 12-13; Corbis: Bettmann, 10 (bottom), 11 (bottom), Peter Turnley, 29 (bottom left); Getty Images: Bert Hardy, 11 (top), Buyenlarge, 10 (inset); Naval History & Heritage Command/U.S. Navy map, 13 (inset); PEOSoldier, 20 (bottom); Shutterstock: arimdambanerjee, 26, Konstantnin, 20 (top), Vartanov Anatoly, 21 (middle); U.S. Marine Corps photo by Cpl. Benjamin R. Reynolds, 22 (top), Cpl. Dwight A. Henderson, 8-9, Cpl. Eric Quintanillla, 14 (top right), Cpl. Liz Gleason, 19 (top left), Cpl. Mace M. Gratz, cover, Cpl. Marionne T. Mangrum, 29 (bottom), Cpl. Michael Augusto, 23 (bottom), Cpl. Michael S. Cifuentes, 23 (top), Cpl. Richard Blumenstein, 28-29, Cpl. Walter D. Marino II, 14 (top left), 19 (top right), Gunnery Sgt. Kevin W. Williams, 22 (bottom), Gunnery Sgt. Scott Dunn, 22 (middle), Lance Cpl. Bridget M. Keane, 19 (bottom both), Lance Cpl. Codey Underwood, 16-17, Lance Cpl. Crystal Druery, 14 (bottom right), Lance Cpl. Jacob W. Chase, 21 (top), Lance Cpl. Jhonson Simeon, 27 (top), Lance Cpl. Kyle McNally, 29 (top right), Lance Cpl. Matthew Manning, 27 (bottom), Lance Cpl. Michael Ito, 14 (bottom left), Lance Cpl. Pedro Cardenas, 18 (bottom), Lance Cpl. Scott W. Whiting, 6 (bottom), Pfc. Crystal Druery, 18 (top), Pfc. Dalton Precht, 21 (bottom), Pfc. Kasey Peacock, 20 (middle), Sgt. Jose Nava, 14 (background), Staff Sgt. Danielle M. Bacon, 29 (top), U.S. Navy photo by MC3 Jonathan Sunderman, back cover, 24-25, MCSA Daniel J. Walls, 4, Seaman Trevor Welsh, 6 (top)

Design Elements
Shutterstock: Akai37, Darq, Filip Bjorkman, kednert, MIRJANA BANJAC, Paul Stringer, URRRA, Yaraz, zsooofija

Printed in the United States of America in Stevens Point, Wisconsin.
092013 007768WZS14

Table of Contents

First to Fight....4
Marines by 7s....6
Careers in the Marines....8
Marine Corps in the 20th Century....10
Iwo Jima....12
Becoming a Marine....14
Contents of a Marine Recruit's Seabag....16
The Crucible: A Rite of Passage....18
Equipping the Marines....20
The MV-22B Osprey....24
Beyond the Battlefield....26
Marine Special Operations....28
Glossary....30
Read More....31
Internet Sites....31
Index....32

First to Fight

Who does the United States government call in an emergency? The Marines! The United States Marine Corps, a branch of the United States Navy, is a rapid-reaction force. Check out the numbers that back up the U.S. Marines.

In conflicts, a Marine Expeditionary Unit (MEU) is often the first force on the ground. An MEU can be called to action at any moment. An MEU includes 2,200 ground and air combat troops, their commanders, and the logistics crews that provide communications, vehicles, and supplies.

An MEU can go from first alert to action in just 6 hours.

- **hour 1** Marine commanders receive orders.
- **hour 2** Marine commanders and staff develop an action plan.
- **hour 3** Marine ground, aviation, and logistics crews get ready to help with the mission.
- **hour 4** Commander approves the plan and sends out orders for each Marine.
- **hour 5** Marines prepare to move out, loading their gear onto vehicles.
- **hour 6** The first wave of Marines is sent in.

	All Armed Services	Marines	Percentage of total that are Marines
Total Military Personnel	1,431,000	202,441	14%
Officers	234,000	21,307	9%
Enlisted	1,183,200	181,134	15%

"Marines. The Few, the Proud."

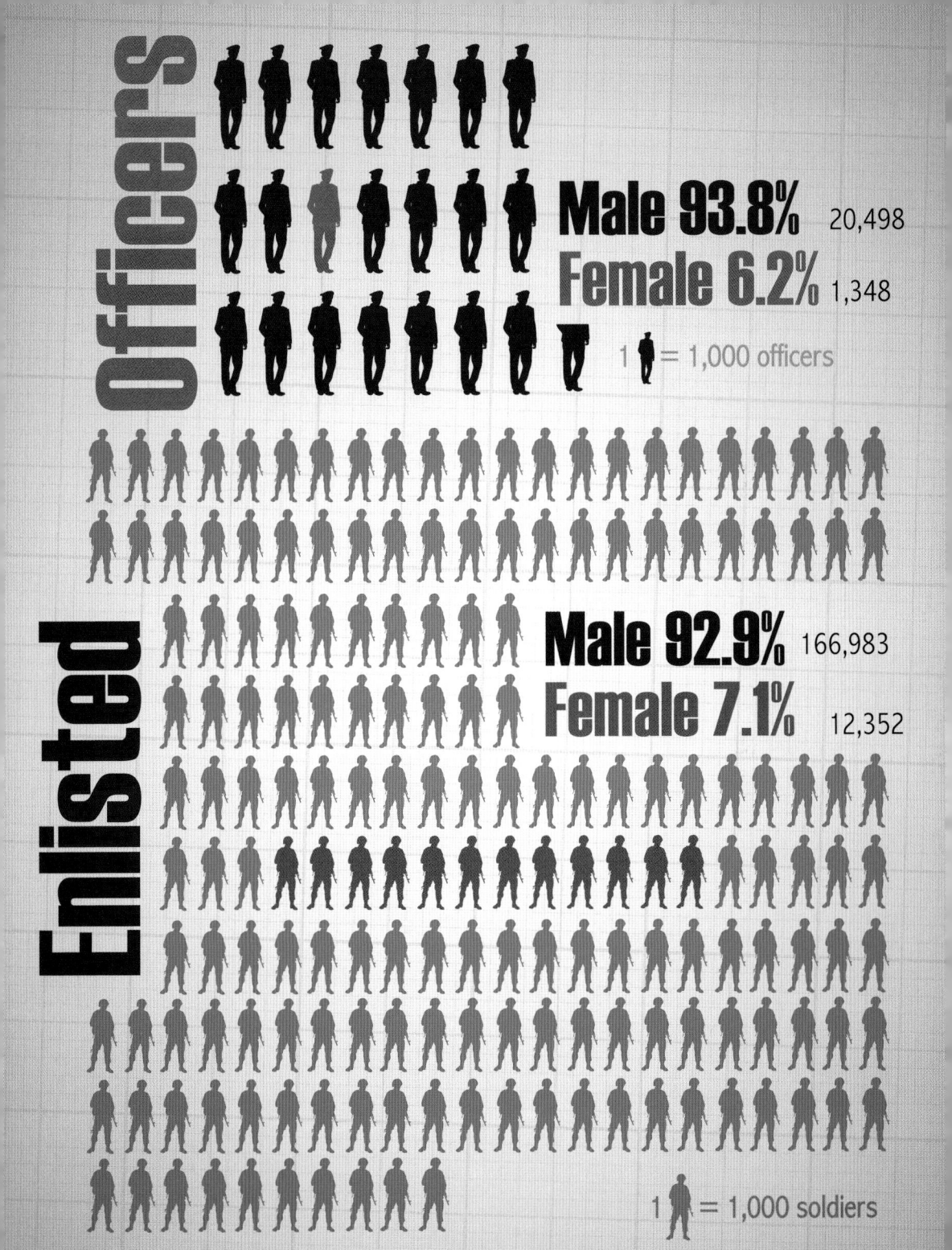

logistics—activities that support fighting units, including transport, supply, communications, and medical aid
aviation—having to do with building and flying aircraft
enlisted—the people in the armed forces who are not officers

Marines by 7s

7

MEUs

ready to respond to a crisis at any time.

7 days

Sun.	Mon.	Tue.	Wed.	Thur.	Fri.	Sat.

a Marine's workweek

7,331

Spouses of Marines who are also in the military

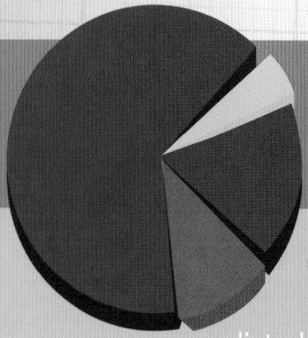

7.6%
enlisted Marines ages 31-35

17.5%
enlisted Marines ages 26-30

7.9 lb.
weight of M27 Marine Infantry Automatic Rifle

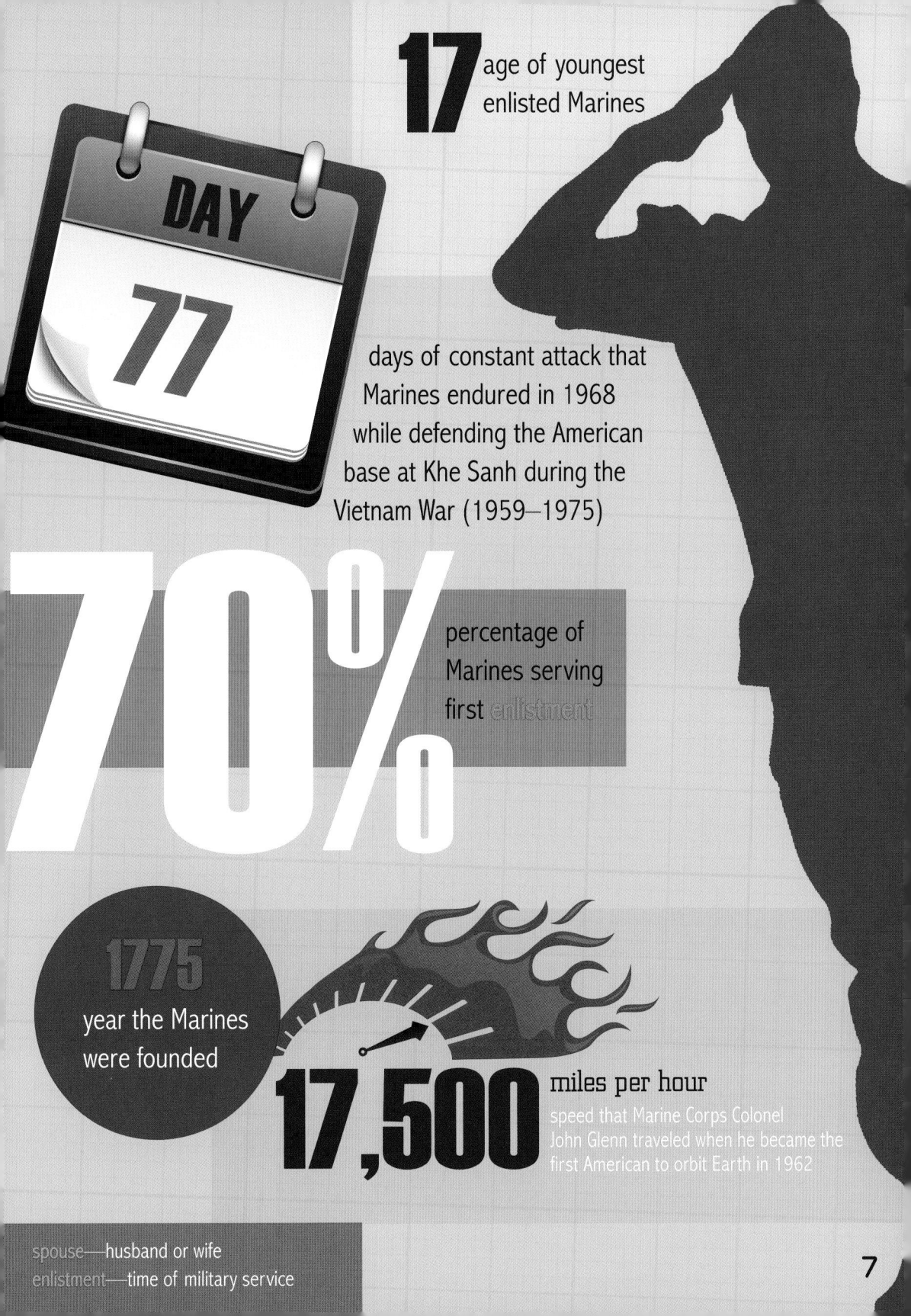

spouse—husband or wife
enlistment—time of military service

Careers in the Marines

Infantry: fighting force

32,749 Infantry Marines (all men)*

*In 2013 the Pentagon lifted its ban on women in combat roles.

42 major job categories

293 specific roles

reconnaissance—a mission to gather information about an enemy
ordnance—military weapons, ammunition, and maintenance equipment

Marine Corps in the 20th Century

U.S. Involvement in World War I (1914–1918)

2 years of major U.S. engagements

9,520 Marines wounded in action

31,600 total Marines serving in war zone

2,461 Marines killed in battle

U.S. Involvement in World War II (1939–1945)

4 years, 8 months of major U.S. engagements

67,207 Marines wounded in action

485,883 Marines serving in war zone

19,733 Marines killed in battle

U.S. Involvement in the Korean War (1950–1953)

4 years of major U.S. engagements

about **130,000**
total Marines serving in war zone

23,744
Marines wounded in action

4,268
Marines killed in battle

U.S. Involvement in the Vietnam War (1959–1975)

Vietnam was the longest and bloodiest war in Marine history.

13,095
Marines killed in battle

88,594
Marines wounded in action

794,000
total Marines serving in war zone

7 years of major U.S. engagements

Iwo Jima

A Great Marine Victory

The Battle of Iwo Jima

Dates: February 19 to March 26, 1945
What: defining World War II battle
Where: Pacific Ocean south of Japan
Goal: capture island of Iwo Jima from Japanese Empire
Result: Japan surrendered the island to the Marines

3 number of Marines pictured in Rosenthal's photo who died in the battle after the flag-raising

2 number of U.S. flags Marines raised atop Mt. Suribachi
1st flag raised: 10:30 a.m.
2nd flag raised: 12 p.m.
The second flag was larger than the first and is the event famously captured by photographer Joe Rosenthal.

About **22,000** Japanese troops dug **11** miles of underground tunnels.

36 days of battle

700 ships transported Marines and cargo to Iwo Jima.

77,000 Marines from 3rd, 4th, and 5th Marine divisions took part in the battle.

Of the **22,000** Japanese soldiers, only about **1,100** survived.

More than **21,000** Marines were wounded.

Nearly **7,000** Marines died.

1/3 of all Marines killed in World War II died on Iwo Jima.

27 Medals of Honor were awarded, **13** posthumously.

Iwo Jima:

8 square miles

4.5 miles long

2.5 miles wide

posthumous—coming or happening after death

Becoming a Marine

Basic Training

The physical requirements of basic training are different for men and women. In all other training, men and women must meet the same standards.

Processing
1 week
medical checkups, physical fitness testing, and getting supplies

Phase 1
4 weeks
physical conditioning; self-defense; marching; Marine Corps customs, history, and values training; weapons training, first aid training

Phase 2
4 weeks
water survival and weapons marksmanship

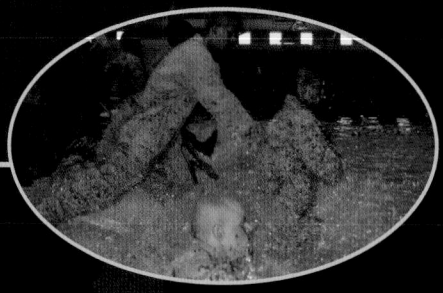

Phase 3
4 weeks
basic warrior skills; defensive driving course; land navigation; basic field skills

Activity
Hours Spent
in Basic Training
487: Eating
13: Marching
572: Sleeping
34.5: Drill practice
41: Academic studies
34: Ethics and values training
54: The Crucible (final testing)
5: On-base liberty on Family Day
60: Senior drill instructor time
106: Free time (includes 4-5 hours on Sundays & holidays)
146: Daily routine (showering, grooming, caring for clothing and room)
81: Physical training/conditioning
225.5: Instruction time (combat, water survival, weapons, field training)

Contents of a Marine Recruit's Seabag

1

- reflective safety belt
- desert cap
- woodland cap
- field desert boonie cap
- green sweatshirt
- pair green sweatpants
- pair combat boots
- pair jungle boots
- pair shower shoes
- pair running shoes
- pair book bands
- hygiene kit
- sewing kit
- green towel
- green washcloth
- flashlight
- jock strap
- mouthpiece
- boot brush
- pair of gloves
- poncho
- cartridge belt
- canteen cup
- Gore-Tex® top
- pillow
- plastic pillowcase
- fabric pillowcase
- mattress cover

2
duffel bags
khaki belts with gold-plated tips
pairs of woodland trousers
woodland blouses
laundry bags
1-quart canteens
canteen covers
blankets
sheets
3
gym trunks
pairs of desert trousers
desert blouses
pairs of white socks
6
undershirts
pairs of brown boot socks
pairs of underwear

The Crucible:
A Rite of Passage

All Marines go through 12 weeks of intense training during boot camp. That training leads up to a final combat exercise called The Crucible.

29: number of problem-solving exercises performed

54: number of hours The Crucible lasts

48: number of miles marched

24: number of logs climbed over and under while carrying supplies

45: pounds of gear carried

36 stations

including exercises such as:

crossing two horizontal cable-supported logs

climbing 8-foot-high horizontal log

working as a team to overcome obstacles in an exercise called 12 Stalls

climbing up and down a 10-foot wall on a knotted rope

crossing 52-foot-long ropes carrying ammunition cans and water cans

retrieving "wounded" dummy from top of 18-foot tower

carrying supplies across two 52-foot-long ropes suspended 2 feet and 10 feet off the ground

Equipping the Marines

Weapons

M16

service rifle
Ammunition: 5.56 x 45 mm rounds
Maximum Range: 3,600 meters
Rate of Fire: 12 to 15 rounds a minute

M203

grenade launcher
Ammunition: 40 mm grenades
Maximum Range: 350 meters
Rate of Fire: single-shot

M249 SAW

automatic weapon
Ammunition: 5.56 x 45 mm rounds
Maximum Range: 3,600 meters
Rate of Fire: 85 rounds a minute

M777 Howitzer

long-range cannon
Ammunition: 155 mm / 39-caliber rounds
Maximum Range: 30 kilometers
Rate of Fire: 5 rounds a minute

M9 Beretta

lightweight pistol
Ammunition: 9 mm rounds
Maximum Range: 50 meters
Rate of Fire: semiautomatic

FGM-148 Javelin

missile
Ammunition: missiles
Maximum Range: 2,500 meters
Rate of Fire: single-shot

Distance

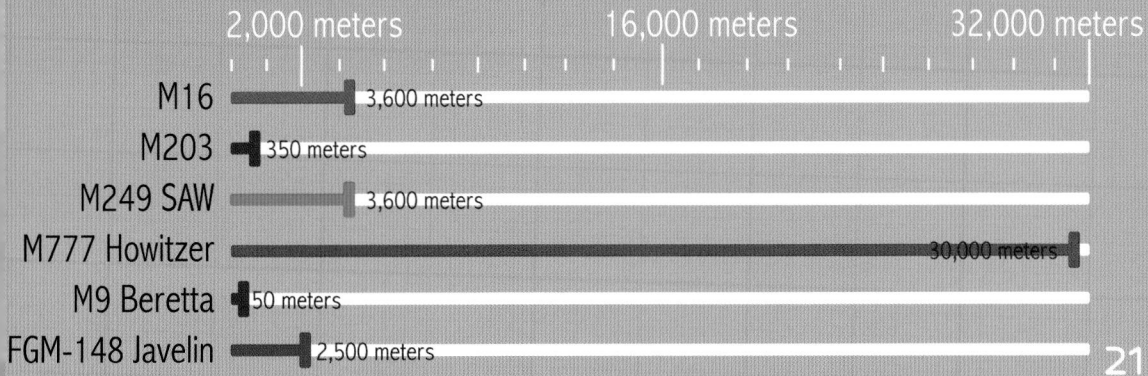

M-ATV

What: all-terrain vehicle
Weight: 25,000 lb.
Size: 20.5 ft. long; 8.2 ft. wide

AAV-7

What: **amphibious** assault vehicle
Weight: 26 tons (fully loaded with a three-man crew)
Capacity: 21 combat-loaded Marines, 3 crew members, 10,000 lb. of cargo

LAV

What: armored fighting tank
Weight: 24,980 lb.
Crew: 3-man crew
Weapons: 2 grenade launchers, 25 mm cannon, two M240 machine guns

Vehicles

amphibious—a vehicle or craft that can travel over land and also over or in water

HMMWV

What: high mobility multipurpose wheeled vehicle
Weight: 5,200 lb.
Special features: armored plating, bullet-resistant glass

MTVR

What: crew and supply transport vehicle
Weight: 7 tons
Capacity: 20 tons

The MV-22B Osprey

The MV-22B Osprey was first used in combat in 2007. It increased the Marines' ability to outmaneuver their enemies. The Osprey has the speed and range of an airplane, but it takes off and lands like a helicopter. It can carry 24 combat Marines from a ship to a land base. The Osprey can go twice as fast and five times farther than previous helicopters.

Weight

52,600 lb.

Cost per unit

$72-$95 million

Wingspan
84.6 ft.
Crew
3
pilot
copilot
crew chief
Range
990 miles
Cruising Speed
322 miles per hour
Capacity
24 combat troops
13
Length
57 ft., 3 in.
Height
22 ft., 1 in.

Beyond the Battlefield

Marine Corps Disaster Relief

The Marine Corps seeks to make the world a safer, better place. Part of that mission involves providing emergency relief when natural disasters hit.

Earthquake in Haiti (January 2010)

The 24th Marine Expeditionary Unit delivered and distributed:

57,368 meals

1,365,617 lb. of rice

589,764 bottles of water

2,781 hand-crank radios

22,064 lb. of medical supplies

79,656 jars of baby food

more than **1,000,000** disaster relief rations

15,207 lb. of other supplies

Flooding in Pakistan

(August 2010)

2,200 Marines responded.

U.S. helicopters rescued **3,075** people.

Marines delivered **650,000** lb. of relief supplies.

Typhoon in the Philippines

(December 2010)

165 tons of relief supplies delivered, including:

500 relief aid boxes

40 generators

250 boxes of blankets

14,500 family ration packs

49,000 lb. of rice

833 sleeping mats

147 bundles of mosquito nets

ration—a family's daily share of food

generator—a machine that produces electricity by turning a magnet inside a coil of wire

Marine Special Operations

Marine Special Operations units are small teams trained to work with foreign armies, defeat terrorists, gather sensitive information, and complete other missions.

Marine Special Operations Command (MARSOC) was activated in 2006. The Marine Special Operations Regiments (MSOR) are combat units based on those used in a 2003 pilot program. In that program, a unit was composed of:

30-man reconnaissance team

29-man intelligence team

7-man combat team

1 headquarters team

Today 2,500 Marines are in Special Operations. Each highly trained unit is sent overseas as needed.

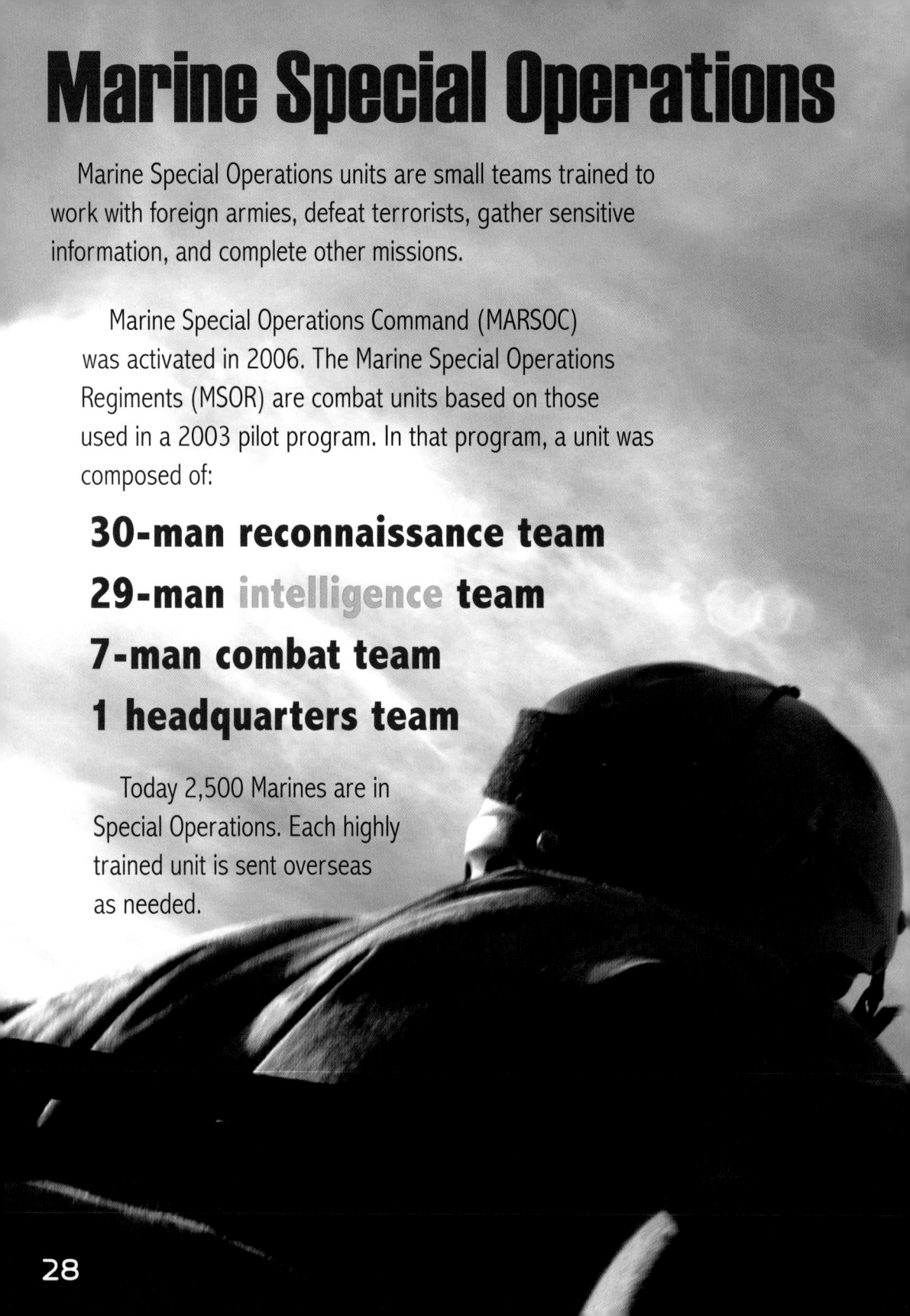

Marine Special Operations Training

Phase 1 10 weeks

swimming, running, **rucking**, hand-to-hand combat, mission planning, fire support, land navigation, combat medic training

Phase 2 8 weeks

intelligence gathering, sea navigation, small boat handling, field training in **urban** and non-urban environments

Phase 3 5 weeks

close-quarters combat, marksmanship, shooting and moving as a team

Phase 4 7 weeks

how to think like the enemy in order to stop acts of terror, **guerilla warfare**, or rebellion

intelligence—secret information about an enemy's plans or actions
ruck—to hike carrying heavy weight in a backpack; ruck is a military term for "backpack"
urban—having to do with a city
guerilla warfare—a type of military action using small groups of fighters to carry out surprise attacks against enemy forces

Glossary

amphibious (am-FI-bee-uhs)—a vehicle or craft that can travel over land and also over or in water

aviation (ay-vee-AY-shuhn)—having to do with building and flying aircraft

enlisted (en-LIS-tuhd)—the people in the armed forces who are not officers

enlistment (en-LIST-muhnt)—time of military service

generator (JEN-uh-ray-tur)—a machine that produces electricity by turning a magnet inside a coil of wire

guerilla warfare (gur-RIL-lah WOR-fair)—a type of military action using small groups of fighters to carry out surprise attacks against enemy forces

intelligence (in-TEL-uh-jenss)—secret information about an enemy's plans or actions

logistics (luh-JIS-ticks)—activities that support fighting units, including transport, supply, communications, and medical aid

ordnance (ORD-nuhnss)—military weapons, ammunition, and maintenance equipment

posthumous (POHST-chuh-muhss)—coming or happening after death

ration (RASH-uhn)—a family's daily share of food

reconnaissance (ree-KAH-nuh-suhnss)—a mission to gather information about an enemy

ruck (RUCK)—to hike carrying heavy weight in a ruck or backpack

spouse (SPOUSS)—husband or wife

urban (UR-buhn)—having to do with a city

Read More

Sandler, Michael. *Marine Force Recon in Action.* Special Ops. New York: Bearport Pub., 2008.

Schwartz, Heather E. *Women of the U.S. Marine Corps: Breaking Barriers.* Women in the Armed Forces. Mankato, Minn.: Capstone Press, 2011.

Sodaro, Craig. *The U.S. Marines Special Operations Regiment: The Missions.* American Special Ops. North Mankato, Minn.: Capstone Press, 2013.

Internet Sites

FactHound offers a safe, fun way to find Internet sites related to this book. All of the sites on FactHound have been researched by our staff.

Here's all you do:

Visit *www.facthound.com*

Type in this code: 9781476539195

Check out projects, games and lots more at
www.capstonekids.com

Index

aircraft, 4, 27
  MV-22B Osprey, 24–25
careers, 8–9
disaster relief, 26–27
gear, 4, 16–17, 18
Glenn, John, 7
history, 7, 10–13, 14
Korean War, 11
Marine Expeditionary Units (MEUs), 4, 6, 26
Marine Special Operations, 28–29
Medals of Honor, 13
officers, 4, 5
Rosenthal, Joe, 12
terrorism, 28, 29
training, 14–15, 29
  The Crucible, 15, 18–19
vehicles, 4, 9, 22–23
Vietnam War, 7, 11
weapons, 6, 9, 14, 15, 20–21, 22–23
World War I, 10
World War II, 10
  Battle of Iwo Jima, 12–13

Titles in this set:

U.S. AIR FORCE by the Numbers

U.S. MARINES by the Numbers

U.S. ARMY by the Numbers

U.S. NAVY by the Numbers